Nan Grandmother Nani Ama Geema T
Grandmama Ba Memere Bomma B
eema Gee Ninny Goma Grambo Av
Tutu Grammie Baba Babushka Mama
Ommy Nonna Amma Gramms Gr
Ya Lao Ye Lita Anya Lolo Gram Yaya Gma Ya Lao Ye Lita Anya Lolo Gram Y
n Uelita Busia Umakhulu Lolly Mami Nan Uelita Busia Umakhulu Lolly
Gee Mawmaw Mémé Gran Mimi GraGra Gee Mawmaw Mémé Gran Mimi
a MomMom Mormor Nai Nai Toots Nana MomMom Mormor Nai Nai T
Ba Nanna GranGran Nanny Ugogo Oma Ba Nanna GranGran Nanny Ugo
Safta Omi Mimzy Maman Grandma Lola Safta Omi Mimzy Maman Grand
Ya Farmor Abby Grandmommy Abuelita Ya Farmor Abby Grandmommy
Nan Grandmother Nani Ama Geema Tita Nan Grandmother Nani Ama Gee
y Grandmama Ba Memere Bomma Bubby Grandmama Ba Memere Bom
eema Gee Ninny Goma Grambo Avó Meema Gee Ninny Goma Gramb
Tutu Grammie Baba Babushka Mamaw Tutu Grammie Baba Babushka
y Ommy Nonna Amma Gramms Granny Ommy Nonna Amma Gramm
Ya Lao Ye Lita Anya Lolo Gram Yaya Gma Ya Lao Ye Lita Anya Lolo Gram Y
an Uelita Busia Umakhulu Lolly Mami Nan Uelita Busia Umakhulu Lolly
Gee Mawmaw Mémé Gran Mimi GraGra Gee Mawmaw Mémé Gran Mimi
a MomMom Mormor Nai Nai Toots Nana MomMom Mormor Nai Nai T
Ba Nanna GranGran Nanny Ugogo Oma Ba Nanna GranGran Nanny Ugo
Safta Omi Mimzy Maman Grandma Lola Safta Omi Mimzy Maman Grand
Ya Farmor Abby Grandmommy Abuelita Ya Farmor Abby Grandmommy
Nan Grandmother Nani Ama Geema Tita Nan Grandmother Nani Ama Gee
y Grandmama Ba Memere Bomma Bubby Grandmama Ba Memere Bom
Meema Gee Ninny Goma Grambo Avó Meema Gee Ninny Goma Gramb
Tutu Grammie Baba Babushka Mamaw Tutu Grammie Baba Babushka
y Ommy Nonna Amma Gramms Granny Ommy Nonna Amma Gramm
Ya Lao Ye Lita Anya Lolo Gram Yaya Gma Ya Lao Ye Lita Anya Lolo Gram Y
an Uelita Busia Umakhulu Lolly Mami Nan Uelita Busia Umakhulu Lolly
Gee Mawmaw Mémé Gran Mimi GraGra Gee Mawmaw Mémé Gran Mim
a MomMom Mormor Nai Nai Toots Nana MomMom Mormor Nai Nai T
Ba Nanna GranGran Nanny Ugogo Oma Ba Nanna GranGran Nanny Ug
Safta Omi Mimzy Maman Grandma Lola Safta Omi Mimzy Maman Gran
Ya Farmor Abby Grandmommy Abuelita Ya Farmor Abby Grandmommy
Nan Grandmother Nani Ama Geema Tita Nan Grandmother Nani Ama Ge

GRANDMOTHER'S MEMORIES

A KEEPSAKE JOURNAL

This journal was given with gratitude to my grandmother

_____

by her loving grandchild(ren)

_____

A SPECIAL NOTE TO GRANDCHILDREN

Grandmothers are simply the best. It's a well-known fact. No one gives better hugs, brighter smiles, or more helpful advice. (And cookies, if you are lucky.) So how do you let your grandmother know how much you really appreciate her? One way is by giving her this special memory journal. There are prompts on its pages to help her tell her story, from the upper branches of her family tree all the way down to you. You will find out secrets, learn about family traditions, and appreciate what makes your grandmother such a treasure. You can read the journal together and ask even more questions about your grandmother's life and your place in a loving family. The memories and wisdom that your grandmother will share will make a wonderful and unique keepsake for you. The greatest gift a grandmother gives is her love, and each page will remind you of that. We sincerely hope you will enjoy giving and receiving this journal.

CONTENTS

MY FAMILY TREE

My Great-Grandmother

My Great-Grandmother

My Great-Grandfather

My Great-Grandfather

My Grandmother

My Grandfather

My Mother

Me

My Sibling

My Sibling

My Great-Grandmother

My Great-Grandmother

My Great-Grandfather

My Great-Grandfather

My Grandmother

My Grandfather

My Father

My Sibling

My Sibling

My Sibling

Chapter One

OUR
FAMILY STORY

LOOK BACK, LEARN, AND LOVE

A FAMILY BEGINS

Our family names are _____

_____

_____

_____

Here's what I know about our family names: _____

_____

_____

_____

_____

Our relatives came from _____

_____

_____

_____

_____

I learned about them through _____

_____

_____

_____

_____

Some traditions we followed as a family were _____

_____

_____

_____

_____

Here is an amazing story from our family's history: _____

_____

_____

_____

_____

We are the accumulation of
the dreams of generations.

STEPHEN ROBERT KUTA

YOUR
GREAT-GREATS

My grandparents were named _____

_____

_____

But I called them _____

_____

_____

This is my own grandmother's story: _____

_____

_____

_____

_____

_____

_____

_____

My other grandparent has a story, too: _____

_____

_____

_____

_____

_____

_____

This is how they met, where they lived, and what they did: _____

_____

_____

_____

_____

_____

_____

_____

A great-grandparent's heart
is a patchwork of love.

UNKNOWN

Something I'd like to tell you about my grandmother is _____

_____

_____

_____

_____

_____

_____

Words I would use to describe my other grandparent: _____

_____

_____

_____

_____

Things I remember the most about my grandparents: _____

_____

_____

_____

_____

_____

_____

_____

Ways you remind me of them: _____

_____

_____

_____

_____

_____

_____

_____

YOUR GREATS

My parents were named _____

_____

_____

But I called them _____

_____

_____

My brothers and sisters were _____

_____

_____

This is my mother's story: _____

_____

_____

_____

_____

This is my other parent's history: _____

_____

_____

_____

_____

_____

They met when _____

_____

_____

_____

The places they lived were _____

_____

_____

_____

_____

If nothing is going well,
call your grandmother.

ITALIAN PROVERB

My parents' jobs were _____

_____

And _____

_____

But they really enjoyed doing _____

_____

And _____

_____

Here's what our family life was like: _____

_____

_____

_____

_____

_____

_____

One thing our family loved to do together was _____

_____

_____

What I'd like you to know about my mother: _____

_____

_____

What I want to share about my other parent: _____

_____

_____

_____

The things they passed down to me were _____

_____

_____

A memory to share from when I was your age: _____

_____

_____

_____

_____

WHEN I
WAS BORN

I was born on _____

_____

The day of the week was _____

_____

In a place called _____

_____

_____

My full name is _____

_____

My parents chose it because _____

_____

_____

_____

_____

As a baby I was _____

_____

_____

_____

_____

_____

_____

Here are the people who lived with us, and their dates of birth: _____

_____

_____

_____

_____

_____

_____

_____

Every house needs a grandmother in it.

LOUISA MAY ALCOTT

Chapter Two

ALL ABOUT ME

MY STORY TO SHARE WITH YOU

WHERE THE HEART IS

The place I lived when I was a little girl was _____

_____

_____

_____

_____

_____

My first memories of home were _____

_____

_____

_____

_____

_____

_____

_____

_____

Let me tell you about my room: _____

_____

_____

_____

_____

We had pets named _____

_____

_____

_____

_____

Something yummy we ate together was _____

_____

_____

_____

_____

Home is people, not a place. If you go back there after the people are gone, then all you can see is what is not there anymore.

ROBIN HOBB

The friends I played with were _____

_____

_____

_____

_____

My favorite things to do were _____

_____

_____

_____

I loved going to the _____

_____

_____

_____

_____

The best place to hide was _____

_____

_____

_____

Here is a story from when I was little: _____

_____

_____

_____

_____

_____

_____

_____

_____

_____

_____

_____

_____

_____

_____

_____

_____

_____

_____

STARTING SCHOOL

My first day at school was _____

_____

_____

_____

The school was called _____

_____

_____

_____

_____

Here's how I got there: _____

_____

_____

_____

_____

My first teacher was called _____

_____

_____

_____

_____

My favorite school outfit was _____

_____

_____

_____

_____

And I always carried _____

_____

_____

_____

_____

You're off to great places! Today is your day. Your mountain is waiting, so get on your way.

DR. SEUSS

Memories from my earliest years at school:

_____

_____

_____

_____

_____

_____

_____

_____

_____

_____

_____

_____

_____

_____

_____

_____

_____

MOVING UP

I started middle school in _____

_____

_____

_____

My school was named _____

_____

_____

_____

_____

The subjects I liked learning were _____

_____

_____

_____

_____

And the ones I didn't like so much were _____

_____

_____

_____

_____

Everybody said I was good at _____

_____

_____

_____

_____

My best friends were _____

_____

_____

_____

_____

If you imagine it, you can achieve it. If you can dream it, you can become it.

WILLIAM ARTHUR WARD

Let me tell you some stories from this time:

_____

_____

_____

_____

_____

_____

_____

_____

_____

_____

_____

_____

_____

_____

_____

_____

_____

SCHOOL'S OUT

The things I liked to do after school were _____

_____

_____

_____

_____

_____

_____

My hobbies were _____

_____

_____

_____

_____

_____

_____

When I was naughty and when I was nice: _____

_____

_____

_____

_____

_____

The best snacks were _____

_____

_____

_____

My after-school friends were named _____

_____

_____

_____

You do not find the happy life, you make it.

CAMILLA EYRING KIMBALL

Weekends were special because _____

_____

_____

_____

_____

_____

During winter breaks I used to _____

_____

_____

_____

_____

_____

I looked forward to summer vacation because _____

_____

_____

_____

_____

_____

My best vacation was _____

_____

_____

_____

_____

_____

_____

_____

This is how I loved to spend my ideal day out of school: _____

_____

_____

_____

_____

_____

_____

_____

HELLO, HIGH SCHOOL

I went to high school at _____

_____

_____

The subjects I enjoyed most were _____

_____

_____

_____

I spent a lot of time watching the clock in this class: _____

_____

_____

_____

My friends were _____

_____

_____

_____

We liked to _____

_____

_____

_____

My school activities included _____

_____

_____

_____

My favorite after-school snack was _____

_____

_____

My go-to outfit for school _____

_____

_____

_____

High school is about finding out who you are, because that's more important than trying to be someone else.

NICK JONAS

Here's how I would describe myself during
my high school years:

_____

_____

_____

_____

_____

_____

_____

_____

_____

_____

_____

_____

_____

_____

_____

_____

MY TIME AS A TEENAGER

When I was a teenager, I was crazy about _____

_____

_____

_____

My favorite kind of music was _____

_____

_____

_____

_____

I used to listen to it on my _____

_____

_____

_____

_____

An instrument I learned how to play: _____

_____

_____

_____

_____

The songs that spoke to me as a teenager: _____

_____

_____

_____

_____

Musicians I loved and went to see were _____

_____

_____

_____

_____

It takes courage to grow up and
become who you really are.

E.E. CUMMINGS

The best books and authors were _____

_____

_____

_____

_____

_____

My favorite character from a book was _____

_____

_____

_____

_____

_____

Some of the movies I loved were _____

_____

_____

_____

_____

_____

My favorite movie theater snack _____

_____

_____

_____

_____

My favorite television shows were _____

_____

_____

_____

_____

I never, ever missed an episode of _____

_____

_____

_____

_____

_____

My best friends were _____

_____

_____

_____

_____

Like most teenagers, we used to wear _____

_____

_____

_____

_____

One thing I will never wear again is _____

_____

_____

_____

_____

How I wore my hair: _____

_____

_____

_____

_____

The things we thought were cool were _____

_____

_____

_____

_____

But definitely not _____

_____

_____

_____

_____

_____

My favorite way to spend time was _____

_____

_____

_____

I had jobs like _____

_____

_____

_____

Someone who had a big influence on me was _____

_____

Because _____

_____

_____

_____

If you met me as a teenager, you would see _____

_____

_____

_____

The bravest thing I did was _____

_____

_____

_____

_____

Here's a secret your parents might not even know about me: _____

_____

_____

_____

_____

Here's something important I learned when I was a teenager: _____

_____

_____

_____

_____

_____

_____

HIGHER LEARNING

I went to college at _____

_____

_____

_____

I chose this college because _____

_____

_____

_____

_____

_____

My college tuition at the time cost _____

_____

_____

_____

I went to school to study _____

_____

_____

_____

_____

_____

_____

I got a degree in _____

_____

_____

_____

_____

_____

Some people get an education
without going to college.
The rest get it after they get out.

MARK TWAIN

My best friends in college were _____

_____

_____

_____

_____

_____

One of my most memorable experiences was _____

_____

_____

_____

_____

_____

_____

_____

_____

_____

_____

Something I learned about myself I didn't know: _____

_____

_____

_____

_____

_____

_____

_____

Advice I would give you about going to college: _____

_____

_____

_____

_____

_____

_____

_____

Chapter Three

MAKING
MEMORIES

LIFE ON MY OWN

ON MY WAY

Here's what I did after finishing school: _____

_____

_____

_____

_____

_____

_____

My new home was in _____

_____

_____

_____

_____

_____

_____

The things that were important to me were _____

_____

_____

_____

_____

_____

The hopes and wishes I had for the future were _____

_____

_____

_____

_____

_____

_____

You'll miss the person you are now
at this time and this place, because you'll
never be this way ever again.

AZAR NAFISI

How I stayed in touch with my parents: _____

_____

_____

_____

_____

_____

The first thing I did when returning to my childhood home was _____

_____

_____

_____

_____

_____

How living on my own helped me to understand my family better: _____

_____

_____

_____

_____

_____

Here's something I learned from that time to share with you: _____

_____

_____

_____

_____

_____

_____

_____

_____

_____

_____

_____

_____

_____

_____

_____

_____

_____

CLIMBING THE LADDER

My first grown-up job was _____

_____

_____

_____

This is what I did: _____

_____

_____

_____

_____

This is how much I made a week or a month: _____

_____

_____

_____

Some of the best things about the job were _____

_____

_____

_____

_____

_____

_____

_____

But to be honest I could have done without the _____

_____

_____

_____

_____

_____

A new job is like a blank book and you are the author.

UNKNOWN

Every job is a learning experience, and I found out that

_____

_____

_____

_____

_____

The next jobs I held were _____

_____

_____

_____

_____

One job that I will never forget was _____

_____

_____

_____

_____

_____

What I was really hoping to do was _____

_____

_____

_____

_____

_____

_____

_____

If I could go back and change something about that time, it would be _____

_____

_____

_____

_____

_____

_____

_____

MAKING A HOME

How I felt making my own home for the first time: _____

_____

_____

_____

_____

Where I lived was _____

_____

_____

How much my rent or mortgage was: _____

_____

_____

The view from my window was _____

_____

_____

My favorite room was _____

_____

_____

Something I brought from my parents' house was _____

_____

_____

A keepsake I still have from that time is _____

_____

_____

Some of the other places I lived were _____

_____

_____

I started to feel like a grown-up when _____

_____

_____

The ache for home lives in all of us.

MAYA ANGELOU

GOOD TIMES

Here's how I loved to spend my free time: _____

_____

_____

_____

Would you find me outdoors or in? _____

_____

My social life was _____

_____

_____

_____

Good friends included _____

_____

_____

_____

The places I loved to visit were _____

_____

_____

_____

My top three movies were _____

_____

_____

_____

Three favorite songs I played on repeat: _____

_____

_____

_____

Bet you didn't know I could dance the _____

_____

_____

*Happiness comes out of being willing
to do your work in your twenties,
to find out who you are, what you love.*

CANDACE BUSHNELL

I never left home without _____

_____

_____

_____

My go-to weekend outfit was _____

_____

_____

_____

And one I'd rather not be seen in now was _____

_____

_____

_____

I got around by _____

_____

_____

_____

Something new I tried or learned was _____

_____

_____

_____

_____

_____

_____

_____

No weekend was complete without _____

_____

_____

_____

_____

_____

_____

LOVE IS
ALL YOU NEED

Where and when I first met my partner/spouse: _____

_____

_____

The first thing I noticed was _____

_____

_____

_____

_____

Here's the true story of how we met: _____

_____

_____

_____

_____

_____

Our very first date was _____

_____

_____

_____

_____

_____

There was a second date because _____

_____

_____

_____

_____

We dated for _____

_____

_____

*The best thing to hold onto
in life is each other.*

AUDREY HEPBURN

The most fun we had together was _____

_____

_____

_____

_____

_____

_____

_____

One time I'd rather forget was _____

_____

_____

_____

_____

_____

_____

When I first met my partner's/spouse's family _____

_____

_____

_____

_____

_____

The moment I fell in love: _____

_____

_____

_____

_____

_____

How we committed to each other: _____

_____

_____

_____

_____

_____

TYING THE KNOT

Where and when we made it official: _____

_____

_____

_____

Some of our guests were _____

_____

_____

_____

Let me tell you about what we wore: _____

_____

_____

_____

The things I will remember forever about that day are _____

_____

_____

_____

_____

Something funny also happened that day: _____

_____

_____

_____

_____

Our hopes and dreams for a life together were _____

_____

_____

_____

_____

*True love stands by
each other's side on good days,
and stands closer on bad days.*

UNKNOWN

A LIFE TOGETHER

How our life together began: _____

_____

_____

Our first home together was _____

_____

_____

We were best friends with _____

_____

_____

_____

Some of the things we liked to do were _____

_____

_____

_____

How being together changed me: _____

_____

_____

_____

_____

Here is a story from that special time: _____

_____

_____

_____

_____

_____

_____

_____

_____

_____

_____

*To love is nothing. To be loved is
something. But to be loved by the
person you love is everything.*

UNKNOWN

Chapter Four

TIMES TO
TREASURE

WELCOMING YOUR PARENT
TO THE WORLD

HELLO, BABY!

When I found out I was pregnant with your parent I felt _____

_____

_____

_____

_____

We were living at _____

_____

We welcomed your parent at _____

_____

_____

The first time we saw your parent we _____

_____

_____

_____

Here's a little bit more about the day your parent was born: _____

_____

_____

_____

_____

_____

We named your parent _____

_____

Because _____

_____

_____

_____

And your parent's nickname was _____

_____

_____

We never know the love of a parent
till we become parents ourselves.

HENRY WARD BEECHER

My memories of your parent as a tiny baby:

_____

_____

_____

_____

_____

_____

_____

_____

_____

_____

_____

_____

_____

_____

_____

_____

STARTING TO GROW

How I would describe your parent as a young child: _____

_____

_____

_____

_____

Other people in your parent's family, before and after, were _____

_____

_____

_____

_____

A person who looked after your parent was _____

_____

_____

_____

Who your parent looked like: _____

_____

_____

_____

What my parents had to say about your parent: _____

_____

_____

_____

_____

Let me tell you how I felt as a new mother: _____

_____

_____

_____

This is a place where grandmothers hold babies
on their laps under the stars and whisper
in their ears that the lights in the sky
are holes in the floor of heaven.

RICK BRAGG

Stories, songs, and books your parent loved are

_____

_____

_____

_____

An activity your parent never got enough of was _____

_____

_____

_____

_____

Places your parent loved to go: _____

_____

_____

_____

Favorite games were _____

_____

_____

_____

Foods your parent found yummy were _____

_____

_____

_____

_____

The best toys were _____

_____

_____

_____

_____

Your parent could not go to sleep without _____

_____

_____

_____

_____

_____

_____

Some of my special memories of your parent as a child
(and some funny and embarrassing ones, too!) are

READY
FOR SCHOOL

Your parent's first school was _____

_____

Here's how I remember the first day: _____

_____

_____

_____

_____

Your parent got to school by _____

_____

_____

After school, your parent always _____

_____

_____

Sports, clubs, and hobbies your parent was involved in:

_____

_____

_____

_____

_____

_____

_____

Let me tell you about your parent's report cards in those early years:

_____

_____

_____

_____

_____

_____

_____

Education is what remains after one has forgotten what one has learned in school.

ALBERT EINSTEIN

GROWING UP

Your parent went to middle school at _____

_____

_____

What your parent liked about school was _____

_____

_____

_____

_____

Something that was not so popular was _____

_____

_____

_____

_____

After school, you could find your parent _____

_____

_____

_____

I remember a funny story from that time: _____

_____

_____

_____

_____

Your parent's best friend was _____

_____

_____

_____

_____

_____

Dreams come a size too big so
that we can grow into them.

JOSIE BISSETT

FAMILY FUN

The things we always did as a family included _____

_____

_____

_____

_____

Our favorite weekends together always had _____

_____

_____

_____

_____

The pets we had were _____

_____

_____

_____

During the summer, we would _____

_____

_____

_____

Here's how your parent got along with the rest of the family: _____

_____

_____

_____

_____

Let me tell you a funny story your parent will never share: _____

_____

_____

_____

_____

_____

Home is where you are loved
the most and act the worst.

MARJORIE PAY HINCKLEY

TEEN TIMES

As a teenager, your parent couldn't get enough of _____

_____

_____

Your parent liked to wear _____

_____

_____

The music coming through the bedroom door was usually _____

_____

_____

And let me describe that bedroom: _____

_____

_____

_____

_____

Your parent made me proud when _____

_____

_____

_____

_____

_____

But I was a little annoyed when _____

_____

_____

_____

Your parent's personality was like yours in this way: _____

_____

_____

_____

_____

It's difficult to decide whether growing pains are something teenagers have or are.

UNKNOWN

Let me tell you all about your parent's experience in high school:

_____

_____

_____

_____

_____

_____

_____

_____

_____

_____

_____

_____

_____

_____

_____

_____

Here are some other stories I'd like to share about when your parent was a teenager:

_____

_____

_____

_____

_____

_____

_____

_____

_____

_____

_____

_____

_____

_____

_____

_____

_____

_____

_____

FLYING
THE NEST

Your parent's dream for the future after school was _____

_____

_____

_____

What your parent did and where: _____

_____

_____

_____

_____

Here is what I remember about the first time your parent left home: _____

_____

_____

_____

_____

What I missed the most was _____

_____

_____

_____

_____

Something I didn't really miss was _____

_____

_____

_____

_____

I knew your parent was really growing up when _____

_____

_____

_____

_____

*Leaving home's a cinch. It's the staying,
once you've found it, that takes courage.*

CATHERINE WATSON

YOUR PARENTS MEET

Your parents met at _____

_____

_____

_____

Here's what happened the first time I met your other parent: _____

_____

_____

_____

_____

What surprised me was _____

_____

_____

_____

_____

I thought this might be a special relationship when _____

_____

_____

_____

_____

_____

Let me tell you a story from the time your parents met: _____

_____

_____

_____

_____

_____

_____

_____

_____

A simple hello could lead
to a million things.

UNKNOWN

Here are my memories about when your parents
decided to make a life with each other:

_____

_____

_____

_____

_____

_____

_____

_____

_____

_____

_____

_____

_____

_____

_____

_____

BIG NEWS

When I found out you were going to be born, I _____

_____

_____

_____

_____

_____

This is how I got the news: _____

_____

_____

_____

_____

_____

_____

When you appeared, I was _____

_____

_____

_____

_____

This is how I first met you: _____

_____

_____

_____

_____

I couldn't help feeling _____

_____

_____

_____

_____

I used to think I was too old
to fall in love again, then
I became a grandparent.

UNKNOWN

Chapter Five

FROM ME TO YOU

BECOMING YOUR GRANDMOTHER

WELCOME TO THE FAMILY

My memories of your first few months are _____

_____

_____

_____

_____

_____

_____

_____

_____

_____

_____

_____

_____

This is how your mother was: _____

_____

_____

This is how your other parent was: _____

_____

_____

A funny question about babies they had for me was _____

_____

_____

_____

This is what it felt like to hold you: _____

_____

_____

_____

_____

Children are the rainbow of life.
Grandchildren are the pot of gold.

IRISH BLESSING

YOU REMIND ME

You were grandchild number _____

_____

The family member you reminded me of is _____

_____

Because _____

_____

_____

_____

I think you looked like _____

_____

Because _____

_____

_____

_____

Here are the ways you remind me of your own parent: _____

_____

_____

_____

_____

_____

_____

_____

_____

_____

_____

_____

_____

_____

Grandchildren are the dots
that connect the lines
from generation to generation.

LOIS WYSE

YOU AS A BABY

This is how I would describe you as a baby: _____

_____

_____

_____

_____

_____

Everyone else in the family thought _____

_____

_____

_____

_____

_____

One thing that made your own personality shine through was

_____

_____

_____

_____

_____

One of the best memories from that time is _____

_____

_____

_____

_____

_____

_____

Just when you think you know all that love is, along come the grandchildren.

UNKNOWN

YOUR PARENTS
AS PARENTS

These are the things your mother loved about having a baby:

_____

_____

_____

_____

_____

_____

And your other parent felt _____

_____

_____

_____

_____

_____

_____

If they came to me about advice, it was _____

_____

_____

_____

_____

_____

_____

_____

_____

_____

_____

_____

_____

_____

_____

_____

There are places in the heart you
don't even know exist until
you love a child.

ANNE LAMOTT

ME AS A GRANDMOTHER

This is how I felt about becoming a grandmother: _____

_____

_____

_____

_____

_____

This is what surprised me the most: _____

_____

_____

_____

_____

_____

_____

A special gift I gave you when you were tiny was _____

_____

I chose it because _____

_____

_____

_____

_____

Things I learned as a grandmother, to pass on to you: _____

_____

_____

_____

_____

_____

_____

_____

A garden of love grows in a grandmother's heart.

UNKNOWN

This is a place to collect special memories
between just you and me:

_____

_____

_____

_____

_____

_____

_____

_____

_____

_____

_____

_____

_____

_____

_____

_____

MY HOPES AND DREAMS

After you appeared in our family life, I wanted the most wonderful future for you. This is what I was thinking about:

_____

_____

_____

_____

_____

_____

_____

_____

_____

_____

_____

_____

_____

_____

_____

_____

_____

_____

_____

_____

_____

_____

_____

_____

_____

_____

_____

_____

_____

_____

A grandmother is a little bit parent, a little bit teacher, and a little bit best friend.

UNKNOWN

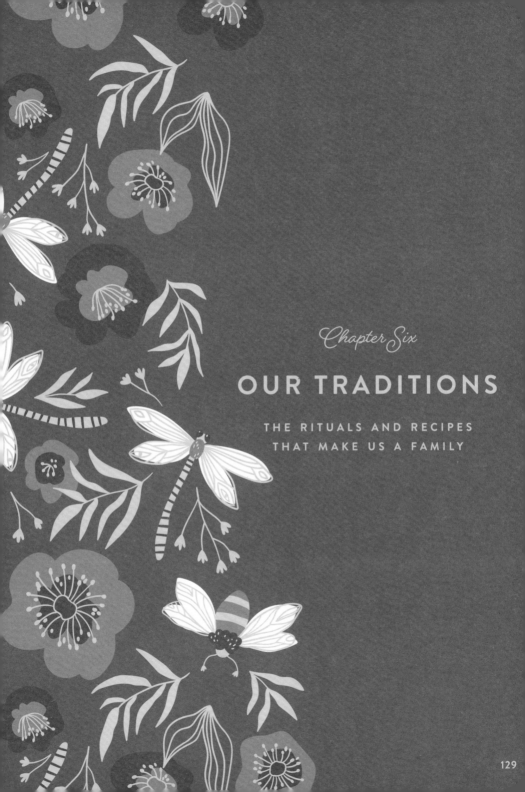

Chapter Six

OUR TRADITIONS

THE RITUALS AND RECIPES
THAT MAKE US A FAMILY

FAMILY HERITAGE

Our family's nationality is _____

_____

_____

_____

Our ethnic background is _____

_____

_____

_____

_____

Here are some of the places your ancestors came from: _____

_____

_____

_____

_____

Some traditions we followed from our ethnic heritage were _____

_____

_____

_____

_____

We also followed these religious traditions: _____

_____

_____

_____

_____

They are important to us because _____

_____

_____

_____

_____

In all of us there is a hunger . . . to know who
we are and where we have come from.

ALEX HALEY

GATHERING
TOGETHER

Our shared family beliefs include _____

_____

_____

_____

_____

_____

_____

Some of the holiday traditions we follow include _____

_____

_____

_____

_____

_____

_____

_____

_____

The holidays that have always meant the most to our family have been

_____

_____

_____

_____

_____

Our family usually gets together when _____

_____

_____

_____

_____

_____

_____

A family is a little world created by love.

UNKNOWN

Let me tell you about some of the amazing times our family got together:

_____

_____

_____

_____

_____

_____

_____

_____

_____

_____

_____

_____

_____

_____

FOOD FOR
THOUGHT

Traditional family dishes that we ate were _____

_____

_____

_____

Something I remember about family meals when growing up: _____

_____

_____

_____

_____

Our family had rules about dinnertime: _____

_____

_____

_____

_____

Some of the foods we ate on special occasions were _____

_____

_____

_____

_____

_____

Here are some family members and their special dishes: _____

_____

_____

_____

_____

_____

_____

_____

_____

_____

Memories are made when
gathered around the table.

UNKNOWN

FAMILY RECIPES

Here are some of the family recipes we've loved to make and eat over the years:

Recipe: _____

Ingredients:

_____   _____

_____   _____

_____   _____

_____   _____

Instructions: _____

_____

_____

_____

_____

_____

_____

_____

Recipe: _____

Ingredients:

_____   _____

_____   _____

_____   _____

_____   _____

Instructions: _____

_____

_____

_____

_____

_____

_____

_____

_____

*There's just so much love that
goes into home cooking.*

MING-NA WEN

SPECIAL
HOLIDAY
RECIPES

On holidays and special times, you could always find on the table:

Recipe: _____

Ingredients:

_____   _____

_____   _____

_____   _____

_____   _____

Instructions: _____

_____

_____

_____

_____

_____

_____

Recipe: _____

Ingredients:

_____   _____

_____   _____

_____   _____

_____   _____

Instructions: _____

_____

_____

_____

_____

_____

_____

_____

_____

_____

_____

_____

_____

MY RECIPE FOR HAPPINESS

Just for you, here is grandmother's recipe for happiness:

Recipe: _____

Ingredients:

_____   _____

_____   _____

_____   _____

_____   _____

Instructions: _____

_____

_____

_____

_____

_____

_____

_____

Recipe: _____

Ingredients:

_____   _____

_____   _____

_____   _____

_____   _____

Instructions: _____

_____

_____

_____

_____

_____

_____

_____

_____

_____

Know your worth.
Believe, tolerate, and allow.

UNKNOWN

⇉Bluestreak

An imprint of Weldon Owen International.

www.weldonowen.com

ISBN: 978-1-68188-641-1

PRINTED IN CHINA

10 9 8 7 6 5 4 3 2 1

Nan Grandmother Nani Ama Geema Tita Nan Grandmother Nani Ama Gee
Grandmama Ba Memere Bomma Bubby Grandmama Ba Memere Bomm
ema Gee Ninny Goma Grambo Avó Meema Gee Ninny Goma Grambo
utu Grammie Baba Babushka Mamaw Tutu Grammie Baba Babushka M
Ommy Nonna Amma Gramms Granny Ommy Nonna Amma Gramm
Ya Lao Ye Lita Anya Lolo Gram Yaya Gma Ya Lao Ye Lita Anya Lolo Gram Ya
Uelita Busia Umakhulu Lolly Mami Nan Uelita Busia Umakhulu Lolly M
Gee Mawmaw Mémé Gran Mimi GraGra Gee Mawmaw Mémé Gran Mimi C
MomMom Mormor Nai Nai Toots Nana MomMom Mormor Nai Nai To
Ba Nanna GranGran Nanny Ugogo Oma Ba Nanna GranGran Nanny Ugog
afta Omi Mimzy Maman Grandma Lola Safta Omi Mimzy Maman Grandn
Ya Farmor Abby Grandmommy Abuelita Ya Farmor Abby Grandmommy A
Nan Grandmother Nani Ama Geema Tita Nan Grandmother Nani Ama Gee
Grandmama Ba Memere Bomma Bubby Grandmama Ba Memere Bomm
ema Gee Ninny Goma Grambo Avó Meema Gee Ninny Goma Grambo
utu Grammie Baba Babushka Mamaw Tutu Grammie Baba Babushka M
Ommy Nonna Amma Gramms Granny Ommy Nonna Amma Gramms
Ya Lao Ye Lita Anya Lolo Gram Yaya Gma Ya Lao Ye Lita Anya Lolo Gram Ya
Uelita Busia Umakhulu Lolly Mami Nan Uelita Busia Umakhulu Lolly M
ee Mawmaw Mémé Gran Mimi GraGra Gee Mawmaw Mémé Gran Mimi C
MomMom Mormor Nai Nai Toots Nana MomMom Mormor Nai Nai Too
Ba Nanna GranGran Nanny Ugogo Oma Ba Nanna GranGran Nanny Ugog
afta Omi Mimzy Maman Grandma Lola Safta Omi Mimzy Maman Grandn
Ya Farmor Abby Grandmommy Abuelita Ya Farmor Abby Grandmommy A
an Grandmother Nani Ama Geema Tita Nan Grandmother Nani Ama Geer
Grandmama Ba Memere Bomma Bubby Grandmama Ba Memere Bomn
ema Gee Ninny Goma Grambo Avó Meema Gee Ninny Goma Grambo
utu Grammie Baba Babushka Mamaw Tutu Grammie Baba Babushka M
Ommy Nonna Amma Gramms Granny Ommy Nonna Amma Gramms
Ya Lao Ye Lita Anya Lolo Gram Yaya Gma Ya Lao Ye Lita Anya Lolo Gram Ya
Uelita Busia Umakhulu Lolly Mami Nan Uelita Busia Umakhulu Lolly M
ee Mawmaw Mémé Gran Mimi GraGra Gee Mawmaw Mémé Gran Mimi C
MomMom Mormor Nai Nai Toots Nana MomMom Mormor Nai Nai Too
Ba Nanna GranGran Nanny Ugogo Oma Ba Nanna GranGran Nanny Ugog
afta Omi Mimzy Maman Grandma Lola Safta Omi Mimzy Maman Grandn
Ya Farmor Abby Grandmommy Abuelita Ya Farmor Abby Grandmommy A
an Grandmother Nani Ama Geema Tita Nan Grandmother Nani Ama Geer